Living

when a loved one has died

Our Thoughts & Love
to all of you as you
face this Holiday season
Bob & Elizabeth
& family

Margaret E. Shepherd
208 S. Washington
Wilmington, IL 60481

*Life and death
are brothers who dwell together.
They cling to each other
and cannot be separated.*

Bahya Ibn Pakuda—*Duties of the Heart*

The author of
Explaining Death to Children
and *Talking About Death: A Dialogue
Between Parent and Child* now
speaks to you, the bereaved adult.

Living
when a loved one
has died

EARL A. GROLLMAN

Beacon Press BOSTON

Copyright © 1977 by Earl A. Grollman

Beacon Press books are published under the auspices of the Unitarian Universalist Association

Published simultaneously in Canada by Fitzhenry & Whiteside Ltd., Toronto

Printed in the United States of America

(paperback)   9   8   7

Library of Congress Cataloging in Publication Data

Grollman, Earl A
   Living—when a loved one has died.
    1. Grief.   2. Consolation.   I. Title.
BJ1487.G73   242′.4   76–48508

ISBN 0–8070–2741–3

To

Gerson S. Grollman

Samuel M. Levinson

Their memory is for a blessing

Contents

This book is about death.
It is written for you who have
sustained the loss of a
loved one—spouse, sibling, child,
relative, or friend.
In your personal diary
    a chapter has ended.

This book is about life.
A new chapter is beginning,
drawing its substance from
the pages that went before.

It is my hope that this book
will help you to manage wisely
the emotions of your grief and will
challenge you to confront
creatively
the death of your beloved.

    A life has ended; living goes on.

SHOCK

Your loved one has died

Everyone dies.

You learned this as a child.

On countless occasions you fantasized
about how you would react when
death strikes.

Your loved one *has* died.
You are unprepared.

The death has struck like
a tidal wave.
You are cut loose from your
moorings.
You are all but drowning in the
sea of your private sorrow.
The person who has been part of
your life is gone forever.

It is final, irrevocable.
Part of you has died.

3   SHOCK

The Sting of Perishable Things

Death diminishes you.
You are living in a nightmare.

You think: "Now I have
touched the bottom of
despair. I can't go any farther."

You do go farther.

There is no comfort.

Absence becomes the only presence.

Too much has been left unsaid,
unfinished, unfulfilled.

There is so much you wanted
to share.
You feel an overpowering desire
to be reunited with
your loved one.
You want to undo this ruthless
separation.

How can you go on living?

Your world is shattered.

You are adrift, alone, in
life's most difficult situation.

You feel utterly lost.

Why?

How often in happy times did
you ask,
    "Why?"

When blessings were yours and
life was joyful, did you ask,
    "Why?"

Now death has shaken your faith,
    "Why?"
    "Why me?"
    "Why didn't I die first?"
    "Why must my life be one of sorrow?"
    "Why?"

There are no pat answers.
No one completely understands
the mystery of death.

Even if the question were answered,
would your pain be eased,
your loneliness less terrible?

There is no answer that bridges
the chasm of irreparable separation.

There is no satisfactory response
for an unresolvable dilemma.

Not all questions have answers.

Unanswered *why*'s are part
of life.

Unsolicited Advice

Everyone knows what is best
for you.
People offer words of consolation:

"I know just how you feel."
 (You want to scream: "No you don't!
 How can you possibly know what
 I'm going through?")

"You are doing so well."
 ("Do you know how I feel
 when you leave?")

"Your loved one lived to a ripe old age."
 ("At any age death is a robber.")

"Others have lived through it."
 ("I'm not concerned about
 others. At this moment I'm
 concerned about myself.")

"It's God's will."
 ("Then this vindictive and vengeful
 God must be my enemy.")

Your heart is breaking—
and they offer you clichés.

You see, they are frightened, too.
They feel threatened and ill at ease.
But they are sharing as best
they can.

Accept their companionship,
but you need not take their advice.

You may simply say, "Thank you
for coming."

And then do what is best for
you.

It's Your Pain Alone

My loved one has died.
It hurts *ME* deeply.
Part of *MY* life has changed.
I don't know what to do.

Notice the words:
    I—ME—MY.
These are the pronouns of grief.
Do not feel ashamed at
constantly referring to yourself.

As Rabbi Hillel said:
    "If I am not for myself,
      who is?"

And It Hurts

When you lose, you grieve.
It is hard to have the links
with your past severed completely.
Never again will you hear
your loved one's laughter.
You must give up the plans
you had made; abandon your
hopes.

Like all people who suffer
the loss of someone they loved,
you are going through a
grieving process.

The time to grieve is NOW.
Do not suppress or ignore your
mourning reactions.
If you do, your feelings will
be like smoldering embers,
which may later ignite and
cause a more dangerous explosion.

Grief is unbearable heartache,
sorrow, loneliness.
Because you loved, grief walks
by your side.

Grief is one of the most basic
of human emotions.
Grief is very, very normal.

But It Hurts . . . Differently

There is no way to predict
how you will feel.

The reactions of grief are
not like recipes,
with given ingredients,
and certain results.

> Each person mourns in a
> different way.

You may cry hysterically,
or
you may remain outwardly controlled,
showing little emotion.

You may lash out in anger against
your family and friends,
or
you may express your gratitude
for their concern and dedication.

You may be calm one moment—
in turmoil the next.

Reactions are varied and
contradictory.

Grief is universal.
At the same time it
is extremely personal.

Heal in your own way.

SUFFERING

The Many Faces of Grief

Your grief is not only frightening
but erratic.

Even though each of us faces
a death in different ways,
we share some points of reference.

You may recognize these feelings:

numbness

denial

anger

panic

physical illness

guilt

depression

These emotions are your
variations on the theme of grief.

If you experience these reactions
you are *not* abnormal.

There is no detour around
bereavement.

Numbness

You are in shock.
Nothing seems real.
You are not there.
People talk to you;
you do not respond.

You feel as though you are
just a spectator.
There is a deadening of feeling.
You have lost your ability to
concentrate.

You have no energy.
There is a slowdown in your speech,
in the way you move.

You are literally stunned.

These are signs of a temporary
paralysis that acts as a
protective mechanism.

Your sensibilities are numbed;
you feel as if you are under
anesthesia.

Because of this numbness,
you do not feel everything
at once;
you have not wholly absorbed
the grim reality of the death
of your loved one.

Denial

"Oh, dear God, it isn't true."

"Not to me!"

"There must be some mistake."

"When I wake up, I'll find
    it didn't really happen."

Secretly you think, or pretend,
that the one you love is still
alive.

You speak of the individual in
the present tense.

Nothing is touched in the room.
Clothes are left intact on the
hangers.

The telephone rings.
For an instant you think it's
your beloved.

Your loved one has not died.
Life will go on as before.

You have not given up hope
that the one you love will
return.

You live in the past,
hoping to bring it back.
To think of the present is
an act of unfaithfulness.

You need time.

Denial and disbelief are initial
reactions to the stress you are
undergoing.

Anger

"Look at my no-good neighbor.
He's in perfect health!
Why didn't he die?
Why did this happen to my
loved one, who was so
wonderful?
What kind of God would
do this to me?
It's all so unfair."

Someone should have helped.

You become annoyed at anyone connected
with the event of death—the physician,
nurse, funeral director, clergy.
You feel you are being punished
and persecuted for a sin you did not
commit.

You reject the overtures of your friends.
How dare they talk of your future
when you know life holds nothing
for you.

You are infuriated with your
loved one for leaving you.
The beloved is "at rest" but
you now have the weight of
the world on your shoulders.

Since you may believe that the
person who died was perfect
and powerful, you wonder why
he or she did not use
extraordinary powers to stay alive.

You are especially enraged with
yourself.
"Why was I not more caring?"
you ask yourself again and again.

Your anger is neither right
nor wrong.

It should be recognized,
not suppressed.
Angry thoughts and feelings
help to express frustrations.
You want to strike out against
those who caused you suffering.

Resentment is a normal part
of your grief process.
As your pain subsides, so
will your anger.

Panic

"What's going to happen
to me?"

Your muscles are tight and
tense.
Your mind races.
You cannot think clearly.
Simple routine decisions
become major problems.

You are emotionally disorganized:

alone,

confused,

helpless,

hopeless.

"If I can't bring my loved
one back, maybe I should
join my love."

Suicide.

"It's crazy even to say
such a thing.
Am I losing my mind?"

No.

Grief has left you drained
and exhausted.
What did you expect?
To fill the void immediately?
To go on living as before?

There is no short cut in
the mourning process.

It must be worked through.

Physical Illness

You are not only mentally upset;
you are physically distressed,
and may experience strange
bodily symptoms:

Nausea

Dizziness

Palpitations

Tightness in your throat

Dry mouth

Sickening sensations in the
pit of your stomach

Rashes

Tension headaches

Back pain

Loss of appetite

Considerable weight loss
or even weight gain

Insomnia

Sighing

Fatigue
"Certain knowledge" that
you now have the same
fatal illness that killed
your beloved. Or that you
will have a similar mishap.

Depressing emotions bring
physical pain.

*As a man thinketh, so
is he.*

Proverbs 23:7

It is your body's response
to bereavement.

Guilt

"If only I had . . .

treated the one I loved
more kindly.

called the doctor sooner.

understood the full extent
of the illness.

taken better care of
him or her.

not lost my temper.

expressed my affection
more frequently."

When death comes, life is
examined.

You become acutely aware of
your failures, real or imagined.
You want to rectify past errors.
You wish to compensate for
the wrongs you have committed.

Some people even punish themselves
with self-destructive acts,
as if to say: "See how much
I am suffering. Doesn't this
prove my great love?"

Self-recrimination becomes a way
to undo all the things that
make you now feel guilty.

And maybe you were guilty.
Perhaps you said things you
should not have said.
Perhaps you neglected to do things
you should have done.
But who hasn't?

What is past is past.
It cannot be changed.
You already have too much pain
to add the burden of self-
accusation, self-reproach, and
self-deprecation.

A wise clergyman once said,
"I believe that God forgives you.

The question is:
        Will you forgive yourself?"

Depression

You no longer care how you look
or dress.
You have no self-esteem.
You must be inept, unworthy.

Since you do not accept yourself, you
feel undeserving of the affection of
your family and friends.
In turn, they don't understand your sudden
unresponsiveness and withdrawal.

You find no pleasure in anything
or anyone.

You feel naked, unprotected.

You have lost interest not only in yourself and those around you, but in life itself.

As you are empty, so is the world around you.

This depression is not weakness.
It is a psychological necessity.
It is one of the slow winding
avenues of sorrow and loss.
It is part of the mournful work of saying
     "Good-by" to your
       beloved.

RECOVERY

Accept Your Loss

Your loved one has not
"gone away on a long journey"
"passed on"
"departed"
"passed away"
"expired."

Your loved one has *died*.

Try to avoid evasions, euphemisms,
fairy tales.

Give up the world of fantasy.

What is—
what cannot be changed—
must be accepted.

Even though it may be the most
difficult thing you have ever done,
you must now face reality.

The denial of tragedy is not
mental health.

Mental health is the recognition
of pain and the attempt to
live with it.

The funeral is over.
The flowers have withered.
Now the loss becomes real.
Your loved one *is dead*.

Can you say the word *dead?*

Try.

Death is a fact, a bitter fact.
Face it.

Oh God,
Give me the courage to change the
things I can change,
the serenity to accept that which I
cannot change,
and the wisdom to distinguish between
the two.

Thomas C. Hart

Express Your Feelings

There are those who will say to you,
"Be strong."
"Be brave."
Don't heed them.

At this moment there is no
virtue in self-control.

It is impossible to handle
rationally your heavy emotional
burdens.

The "brave" ones with the
stiff upper lip may be headed
for trouble.

You want to forget, to escape,
to sleep.

Sedatives, tranquilizers, barbiturates,
stimulants seem to be an easy
way to soothe your agony.

Beware of the medicine chest!

If drugs are prescribed by your
physician, follow his instructions
exactly when you take them.

However, when you are under stress,
moderate usage can soon become excessive.

Do not decide for yourself what
dosages you should take.

Reliance on alcohol can
also be harmful.

Do not substitute drug dependency
for human dependency.

You need to release your emotions.

But you cannot do so if you depend
on narcotics, which can inhibit both memory
and feeling.

Crying is a means by which
you work your way out of the
depths of despair.

Of course your weeping will not
bring back your loved one.
But that's why you cry.
Because you cannot bring your
beloved back to life.

Tears are not evidence of weakness.

When the members of a family, both male
and female, cry together, they are
sharing the inexpressible pain of
separation.

So express your feelings of grief;
allow yourself to show your grief.

Talk It Out

And let there be talk.
Put your feelings into words.
Call your emotions by their
rightful names:

"I am angry."

"I am sad."

"I am hurt."

Say these out loud.
Scream them if you want.
You may feel relief.

Some people like to keep a
diary to record their
feelings on paper.
You may wish to try this.

Repeat over and over again
all the circumstances surrounding
your loss.

Review both pleasant and
unpleasant memories.

Pleasant—because of the love
you shared.
Unpleasant—because every relationship
is tinged with unhappiness as well
as joy.

Talk things out.
Express your feelings.
Act out your grief.

Sorrow, like the river, must
be given vent lest it erode
its bank.

A NEW LIFE

Take Your Time

Life is not fair.
You must find a way
to live with an unfair life—
to live without the one you loved.

How to begin?

Maybe with a complete new start
somewhere that will take you away
from painful memories.

So why not . . .

Sell your house?

Move to another city?

Really start anew?

Wait!

Your judgment is uncertain now.
Getting used to a new life
takes time and thought.

Too many people have impetuously
left their familiar settings only
to find even greater confusion
and uncertainty.

Postpone major decisions if you can.

Walk. Don't run.

*You cannot plant an acorn in
the morning and expect that
afternoon to sit in the shade
of the oak.*

Antoine de Saint-Exupéry

Memories of the Past . . .
A Bridge to the Future

The depth of your sorrow diminishes
slowly and at times imperceptibly.

Your recovering is not an act of
disloyalty to the one who has died.

Nor is it achieved by "forgetting"
the past.

Pictures and mementos may be
tangible reminders of days gone by.

Don't try to destroy a beautiful
part of your life because
remembering it hurts.

As children of today and tomorrow,
we are also children of yesterday.

> The past still travels with us
> and what it has been makes us
> what we are.

But memories are not enough.

You must not become a "slave" to
the past by worshiping at the memorial
shrine that you, yourself, have erected.
You must not think, "Everything's
the same. Nothing has changed."

If you believe that, you are preventing
the building of a bridge to the
future.
You would be living in a world made up
exclusively of memories.

Try to strike that delicate balance
between a yesterday that should
be remembered
and a tomorrow that must be created.

The Medicine of Time

Grief work takes time.
How long?
Much depends upon you and your
relationship to your beloved.

When did your loved one die?
Was there a long illness?
How much help have you been given?

Do you think you are demonstrating
your love by prolonging the length
of your grief?

Because there are many variables,
one person may quickly pick up the
threads and work out new patterns
of behavior,
while another, even after a longer
grieving period, still cannot adjust
to a new life.

You will have many slips and spills
before you feel that your feet are
again on firm ground.

Just when you are making great strides
forward, you receive a startling setback.

It may happen on a holiday, birthday,
anniversary.

Or it may be triggered by your favorite
song being played on the radio.

You think you are back to where it
all started—at the bitter
moment of death.

But remember, anguish, like ecstasy,
is not forever.

"Time heals," many people say.

It may.
It may help to dull your pain.

But the medicine of time,
taken by itself,
is not sure.

Time is neutral.

What helps is what you do with time.

Are you using the time to face up to
the fact that the one you loved is dead?

Are you using the time to give vent
to your fears and anxieties?

Are you using the time to create a
capacity for enjoyment without feeling
guilty?

Are you using the time to build a
life with new friendships?

Is there an upward slope of improvement?

    You must help time to do its healing.

Do Something—
Even Routine Things Will Help

It's hard to begin a new
way of life.

You just can't summon up the energy
or concentration to start afresh.

It's difficult to acknowledge the
letters of condolence and
offerings of sympathy.
Or even to locate a will, or
check insurance policies.

Doing these things is agonizing
because they seem to make
permanent the separation.
You find excuses for not doing
what you must.

Yet you have to,
whether you like it or not.

You are declining invitations to
visit friends.
Are you making excuses to stay
at home?

That's understandable.
Your home is now your haven.
It is secure, isolated, protective.
Staying at home keeps you from
having to face other people.
Since you are uneasy in venturing
out of the house, you withdraw.

But you must recognize that you
are fleeing into loneliness.

The first time that you leave
your house to go to the market
may be a devastating experience.

You may surprise yourself by crying
if the grocer expresses
his sympathy.

But once you have done it,
it is over.

You need not go through the ordeal
with that person again.

You've made it.
You are out of the house.
You continue to exist.

Not like before.
Not the way you would choose—
if you had a choice.

But you are beginning again.

You must now
prepare for the future.
Make a list of activities
for the next few days.

Have a plan.

You don't have to follow it exactly,
but have a plan.
You are confronted with the bitter fact
that you are destined to
go on living.

Life goes on ... I forget just why.

Edna St. Vincent Millay

Live One Day at a Time

Memories—tender, loving, bittersweet.
They can never be taken from you.
Nothing can detract from the joy
and the beauty you and your loved one
shared.

Your love for the person and
his or her love for you cannot be altered
by time or circumstance.
The memories are yours to keep.
Yesterday has ended, though you
store it in the treasurehouse of
the past.

And tomorrow?

How can you face its awesome
problems and challenges?
It is as far beyond your mastery
as your ability to control
yesterday.

Journey one day at a time.
Don't try to solve all the
problems of your life at once.

Each day's survival
is a triumph.

Discovering New Resources
in Yourself

You are doing things you never thought
possible.
You are discovering hidden capabilities
you had never before tapped.

Never before was it necessary for you
to balance the checkbook.
After numerous attempts,
you finally succeed.

"I've never been able to take care
of the maintenance of the house."
You just replaced the blown fuse.
Or put a washer on a leaky faucet.

A sense of inner satisfaction emerges.
"I never thought I could do
so many things.
I've never had to before."

You are becoming less dependent.
You are declaring your independence.
You are making a new adjustment
to life.

Getting out of Yourself

You need diversions,
small variations and changes, such as
physical activity:

> Immersing yourself completely in
> the garden, or
> playing tennis or golf, or
> just walking in the park.

Feelings can be marvelously
released by

    painting,
    reading,
    dancing,
    writing, or
    joining an amateur theater group.

    And travel. An opportunity
    to meet new people,
    see new sights, and
    reassess your life without
    day-to-day pressures.

But be careful in the beginning that
you don't become overly involved in
an endless treadmill of activity.

In periods of stress you need time
to rest your body
and your mind.
You need to be by yourself.

Solitude is not loneliness;
loneliness is the pain of being alone.
Solitude is the glory of being alive.

In solitude you find time to think
and take stock of your life.

Faith and Philosophy

Death is a journey into the unknown.

How you handle your loved one's death
reveals much about how you view life.
Your religion may provide you with
a philosophical base for confronting
moments of darkness and despair.

Religion does not ignore your natural fear
of painful separation.

Rather, your faith offers you a way
to share resources in your encounter
with helplessness, guilt, and
loneliness.

You may find that no event—
even death—
separates you from God.

The funeral involves you in
the meaningful participation
of spiritual values.

Special customs and rituals
can play a vital role in
the healing work of grief.

Support from the religious community
brings a sense of belonging and
comfort.

For many, the belief in an afterlife
helps dull the pain of awareness
of one's finite nature.

Faith offers a source of strength
beyond yourself.

Friends and Others
Who Can Help You

Grief shared is grief diminished.
You are beginning to accept the
companionship of others.
All people need social support.

If you have one close, trusted friend,
you are truly fortunate.

A person who will share with you
the agony of your grief,
so that on your sorrowing path
you do not walk alone.

Accept the strength that can be drawn
from someone who cares about you.

But do not allow anyone
to suffocate you, or
to take over your life.

Still, you may feel deserted.
Some of your old friends
may have "abandoned" you.
After they made their token
condolence call, they seemed
to vanish.
You have not heard from them
since the funeral.

But have you considered that
they may feel threatened and
don't want to hear about grief?
Or that they mistakenly believe that
you want to be by yourself?

Still, you are not alone.

Organizations with people who
suffered similar bereavements
are ready to assist you.

They will listen.

You may find that you need
a different kind of help.

After a period of time,
you don't think that you are
"making it."
You are not in control of yourself.
Depression is deepening.
Bodily distress is becoming worse.
You are more dependent
on drugs or alcohol.
A death wish becomes
more pronounced.

You need assistance.

Contact at once
the physician who takes care of your family,
or a member of the clergy
whom you know and respect,
or a social service organization,
or a mental health clinic.

Getting professional help
is not an admission
of weakness.

It is a demonstration of
your determination and courage.

As You Help Others

Begin to devote some of your energy
to others, not only to yourself.

Those who bring sunshine to others,
cannot keep it from themselves.

Sir James Barrie

There are other people
who have suffered and
who have needs that
you who mourn
can now serve.

There are

    hospitals

    charities

    churches

    that need your help.

You can become
a Big Brother or
Big Sister.

You can read to the blind.

You are not alone
in undergoing
pain and crisis.

    One touch of sorrow
    makes the whole world kin.

At first you have to
force yourself to leave
the security of your house
in order to share somebody else's problems.

Is it worth the effort?
You have enough of your own grief.
Why burden yourself with
the grief of others?

And maybe you will be rejected.

But try.
Offer your services.
See how quickly
you will become
involved.

You will find that
you are important,
you are wanted,
you are needed.

Because you, yourself, have
experienced grief,
you are better able to understand
the heartaches of others.

As you lift a hand to help another,
you are lifting
yourself

Living Remembrances

At one time, men built
palaces of stone,
elaborate mausoleums,
as their way of commemorating
their dead.

There are other ways to perpetuate
the memory of your loved one.
Through your own life
you can prolong the memory.

Death brings you a choice.
It can lead you
to the edge of the abyss.
Or you can build a bridge
that will span the chasm.

Your loved one is still
part of your life.

Whatever it was that
made your beloved dear to you,
you can make real for others.

The memory of the dead
can indeed outlast
the monuments to the dead.

Recovery and Growth

You may not have completely
regained your balance.
Yet life continues, though scars remain.
You are breathing, moving, functioning.
You are now able to remember
the one you loved,
and the circumstances
surrounding the death,
without falling apart.

You had underestimated
your ability to survive.
If there is darkness when you turn back,
there is still enough light
to go forward.

Death has brought you face to face
with your own mortality.
You are looking at this
irrational world
with different eyes.
You gain insights that
had previously escaped you.

That which does not kill me
makes me stronger.

Friedrich Nietzche

You are more aware than before
of what is significant
and what is trivial.

Your beloved lived.
But you're still alive.

The future is worth expecting.

Henry David Thoreau

You have changed.

You have grown.

You understand for the first time
what the Psalmist meant
when he said:
"Yea, though I WALK THROUGH
the valley of the shadow of death."

The important words are
"WALK THROUGH."

You WALK THROUGH.
You do not remain where you were.

Life is for the living.

THE AUTHOR

Earl A. Grollman, rabbi of Beth El Temple in Belmont, Massachusetts, and former president of the Massachusetts Council of Rabbis, is a pioneer in the fields of crisis intervention and thanatology. He is a member of the editorial board of *Omega* magazine and is on the advisory board of the Foundation of Thanatology of Columbia-Presbyterian Medical Center in New York. An author of many books including *Concerning Death, Talking About Death,* and *Explaining Death to Children* published by Beacon Press, he also lectures extensively to both lay and professional audiences throughout the United States.